easy way to be

Easy way to be
Jon Stone Jackson
Copyright © 2024 by Jon Stone Jackson

ISBN 979-8-89383-836-7

easy way to be

Getting A Better Connection With Men

jon stone jackson

one

. . .

THIS IS A GUIDELINE TO PREPARE YOURSELF FOR your king or to be better for the one you already have. Most women don't fully know men and weren't taught how to treat a man properly, so this may help with the disconnect in the relationship. Men are simple and very easy to please, so follow these steps, and I can promise you a positive outcome.

two

. . .

Random acts of appreciation, whether he did something big or something small. Men love being appreciated; feeling appreciated will make him a better version of himself for you. When I say appreciation, I mean verbally telling him you appreciate him and that his hard work isn't going unnoticed. You would genuinely be surprised at how far a few words of encouragement can take you.

three

. . .

WE UNDERSTAND MEN ARE SUPPOSED TO COURT women, and we can never take that away, but men want to feel special sometimes. So plan a date or do something fun you know he would like; it's really the little things that matter the most. Always remember that buying under-clothes is like buying flowers for men.

four

. . .

KNOWING WHEN TO TALK AND WHEN TO LISTEN
will be a huge factor in communication. There
will come a time when talking isn't necessary,
and many women (not all) can't tell the differ-
ence, so it comes off as hazardous. Men love a
peace of mind, despite how tough we may
seem. So that comes with knowing when
talking isn't necessary; the last thing you want
is for him to be there physically but not there
mentally.

five

· · ·

STOP BRINGING UP ANY OLD TRAUMA IN THE relationship. Men hate that if you make a conscious decision to further the relationship, leave everything in the past. That's only making him resort back to the same actions to feel better about himself.

six

. . .

HALFWAY THROUGH THIS BOOK, IT'S GOING TO BE some woman who argues about what they deserve, and men are this and men are that. Please don't be them, woman; this book is solely about getting a better perspective on how men think and the betterment of the relationship. A lot of times, it's a tug-of-war thing instead of pushing forward as one, and that's turmoil in itself.

seven

. . .

THE CRUCIAL PART OF THIS BOOK IS YOUR SEX LIFE. I believe sex is a high percentage of how a relationship may go, and women tend to get complacent or lazy. During sex, you lose the energy to completely please your man or make having sex like a job you hate and instead should be looking at it like a hobby you love. If you and your man live together, stop going to bed with big panties, bonnets, and oversized t-shirts all the time. If men see women at her most attractive throughout the day, it can be disheartening to see his woman in a less flattering light at the end of it. If you don't live with your man, every chance you get, do something to spice the sex life up.

eight

. . .

TRY TO LEARN OR GAIN INTEREST IN THINGS HE likes, whether it's video games, sports, rap videos, etc. This will gain you other things you can bond with regardless of whether you like it or not. That's just another avenue to get more understanding. Whenever a man is happy, it is his vulnerable state, so he is likely to be more open.

nine

. . .

Understanding everything isn't about him cheating. When a guy feels like he's not at his full potential or going through something mentally, emotionally, or financially, he tends to shut down most women, get offended and make it something it's not, and cause unnecessary energy in the relationship when he really needs more support and peace to get to his next chapter.

ten

. . .

KNOWING WHAT BATTLES TO FIGHT: EVERY disagreement doesn't need an argument, even if you are right sometimes. Just let him be to save the peace. I have spoken with numerous older couples in 20- to 30-year relationships, and all say don't stress the little things. You will be surprised at how much tension things like that relieve. As men, we may have certain types of egos, so you may have to feed them from time to time, and I didn't design these rules. I'm just telling you how the male brain operates.

eleven

. . .

IT'S CERTAIN THINGS YOU WOULD NEVER DO IN your relationship at the beginning, so you have to have the same views in the middle of the relationship, the same way you wouldn't really let him see you with your hair any type of way or make sure your panties and bra match should be protocol. You want him to notice your efforts. I hear tons of men say they miss the woman their significant other used to be.

twelve

. . .

THIS ONE IS A VERY BIG ONE, AND WHAT DRIVES most men away in a relationship is nagging. It's one thing a man cannot handle: nagging, the behavior of complaining or finding fault without the intention of finding a solution. I have spoken to many men of all different nationalities, and this was very high on the list.

thirteen

. . .

STAY TRUE TO YOUR FEMININITY. THERE'S NO SENSE in having a strong man contest with a man, or if a man can do it, so can I attitude. Men and women are the exact opposite, so they should do nothing alike. Staying true to your femininity is the highest form of womanhood.

fourteen

. . .

MEN ARE EGOTISTICAL, SO STROKING A MAN'S EGO is another game changer. Give him compliments or good energy on anything he works on. If he is working out, speak about his body looking better. If he just got a haircut, comment on how handsome he looks. Things like that make him feel good, and when he feels good, he will be a better person to you.

fifteen

. . .

I HEAR A LOT OF WOMEN COMPLAIN ABOUT THE lack of communication from men, but are you a good communicator? Healthy communication is not just being willing to talk about it; it has a lot to do with your tone and your delivery. If either one is off, then he won't listen, and you will never get your point across, so try to speak *to* him and not *at* him.

sixteen

. . .

MEN GO THROUGH SO MANY THINGS THAT THEY
don't speak about, so know how to read him so
you can understand his silence. He might need
some breathing room or some time to hiself to
regroup and figure something out. Nothing
personal because it's just certain things you
won't understand about a man, so you have to
let him have some me time.

seventeen

. . .

I HOPE THIS BOOK WAS A BIG HELP AND GAVE YOU a better understanding of how the male mind operates. You have to add it to your daily regimen to get the full return and have an advantage in your relationship.

Made in the USA
Middletown, DE
04 September 2024

59741307R00015